Small Business

The Rookie Entrepreneur's Guide

How To Start Your Own Business

10 Step Action Plan

By Adam Richards

© Copyright 2014 – Adam Richards

ISBN-13: 978-1516954766
ISBN-10: 1516954769

Table of Contents

Introduction 1

Chapter 1: Step One – Idea Generation 3

    Personal Evaluation 4

    Assessment from external sources 5

    Consider all possibilities 6

Chapter 2:   Step Two – Proper And Solid Research 9

    Research that 'industry' 10

    Research your 'target customers' 10

    Research your 'competition' 11

    Make sure you do those 'surveys' 11

    Have those 'focus groups' 12

    Get help 13

Chapter 3: Step Three – The Business Plan 15

    You Must have a concise plan 16

    Make sure that all the key areas are covered 17

    Pay attention to the USP of your business 17

    Pay attention to those sales projections 18

    Executive Summary 19

Chapter 4: Step Four – Getting Your Finances In Order 21

Make sure that you budget your spending 22

Make sure that you invest well 22

Make sure that you maintain those records well 23

Make sure that your personal and business bank accounts are kept separate 24

Cut down on those 'fixed' costs 24

Make sure that you create the right legal structure 25

Make sure you get insurance if you need it 26

Chapter 5: Step Five – Choosing A Business Structure 27

Types of Business Structures 28

Choosing a Business Structure 29

Chapter 6: Step Six - Selecting And Registering Your Business Name 33

Naming your small business 34

Registering your Small Business Name 36

Chapter 7: Step Seven – Necessary Licenses And Permits 39

Business License.. 40

Fire Department Permit...................................... 41

Air And Water Pollution Control Permit.............. 42

Sign Permit... 42

County Permits.. 42

State Licenses.. 43

Federal Licenses.. 43

Sales Tax License... 44

Health Department Permit.................................. 44

Chapter 8:   Step Eight - Location, Location, Location 45

Choose the most 'conducive' location.................... 46

Make sure that it is 'financially' viable.................. 47

Rent 'smart'.. 48

Security.. 48

Make sure that you inspect that property you have selected.. 49

Play smart by locating next to the competition.. 49

Think 'convenience'... 50

Chapter 9: Step Nine - Choosing An Accounting System 51

Narrow down those software choices.................... 52

Industry-specific accounting systems....................53

Talk to others 54

Find out whether it will grow with your business
....55

It should be compatible with your bank...............55

Choosing between online and desk accounting
software 56

Can that access be restricted? 56

Does it come with a free trial?.........................57

Chapter 10: Step Ten - Promoting And
Marketing Your Small Business 59

Give it away for free! 60

Be consistent in that e-mail campaign...................61

Try unusual marketing methods...............................61

Go in for joint promotions with other small
business 62

Create special deals for your existing customers
....62

Offer a premium version of your product or
service...63

Conclusion 65

Introduction

So, you've finally decided to take the plunge and venture into the entrepreneurial boots that have been waiting for you all this while. There's a thing or two that you need to know about the terrain that you will soon be in the process of navigating; it's really a lot rougher than you think it is and if you're not careful, you might just end up wishing that you had never made that foray into the business world, after all.

This book is an attempt to help you ensure that the business you do finally start will be a profit-making machine, much like you always dreamed it would be. It will help you ensure that you take just the right 'steps' towards tailoring that business of yours for success, overcoming all the tiny obstacles that come in your way, that cumulatively have a rather gargantuan effect in restraining you to reach your full business potential. Think of it as a guide towards creating the lucrative small business, you always dreamed of.

In the end it is experience that we all must make a point of learning from; the great part about having this invaluable book is that you get all the experience you need without even having to make the mistakes that you would otherwise have to make in the process of garnering that high level of experience. You will learn how to do the 'right' things and not the wrong ones when it comes to the process of planning and setting up that business of yours, ensuring that you are well on the path to unbridled success in the realm of your small business.

Let's begin, then, and 'climb that staircase' step by step, towards entrepreneurial success!

Chapter 1:

Step One – Idea Generation

One might think that it would be absolutely essential to have a great idea as far as it comes to setting up a business that will reap great dividends over time, right? Well, you couldn't be further from the truth if you thought the same. In fact, some of the best ideas are really the most common ones – the tried and tested, the ones that actually work.

All you need to do is take a great idea that is already existing out there, and then put an entirely new spin on it so that you pack a punch where it comes to achieving success in your work out there. In fact, by doing so you are really creating your own unique business idea. Let's take a look, then, at the process of idea generation and all that it entails in order to make it successful!

Personal Evaluation

This is extremely important when it comes to the successful idea generation for your business. At first you must take out the desired amount of time to actually spend on brainstorming what you are truly passionate about. Once you have found out the same, you have to see if your skill sets matches up to the 'idea' that you have thought of; it might not be a very good idea to pursue something that you might not be best equipped to do.

Once you have aligned your skill sets with the idea that you imagine could catapult you to entrepreneurial fame, you have to see if there is a real 'need' out there for the product or service that you are proffering to offer. If there is, you know that you are headed in the right direction!

Assessment from external sources

You might wish to look up to people like peers and your family in order to get the best possible advice as to whether the business idea you have chosen in the point above, is really indeed most worthy of the merit that you have bestowed upon it, or not.

You have to understand that by doing this you get an unbiased 'outside perspective' on your proposed business idea in the form of things like constructive criticism that might go a long way in ensuring that your idea does indeed hold water and that you are well poised towards launching your new venture. You might wish to talk to a few entrepreneurs as well; they have been there and done that and they will most certainly be able to offer you the best possible advice on how to take that idea of yours forward in the smoothest manner possible.

Consider all possibilities

The very fact that you have a brilliant idea does in no way imply that you are 'sorted' when it comes to being on the path to entrepreneurial success. You have to understand that there will be a lot of hurdles along the way, which could indeed lead to a lot of disappointment should things go askew in the process of setting up that business. Of course you need to be mentally prepared for the same; the last thing you want is to be discouraged by the potential hurdles that come along your path, to the point where you want to throw it all away.

By being apprised of the hurdles that might come along, you are preparing yourself to be a lot more resilient than you otherwise would have been, thus paving the way for you to face any obstacle that might come your way. In fact, some of the most successful entrepreneurs out there are those that have embraced failure time and again, simply because they believed to the core in the ideas that they felt would change the world.

Of course it is vital that you have a great business idea to begin with. Sometimes you might just get that 'Eureka!' moment when you're sitting in a mall and observing things around you. But in addition to the pointers that we have discussed, one also needs to do a thorough amount of research into the idea that they have stumbled upon, in order to assess its viability in the market out there. The following chapter is an endeavor in just that. Let's take a look!

Chapter 2:

Step Two – Proper And Solid Research

Of course you must do an adequate amount of research into that small business idea of yours that you believe is going to reap 'big' dividends for you. Not doing so would only be akin to walking in the dark. Let's take a look, then, at how we can do the requisite amount of research that is required to literally 'confirm' that business idea of ours while at the same time lighting the path that will take it to fruition.

Research that 'industry'

Make sure that you 'research' your industry well. Of course the goal would be to 'research here', but it must be specific towards the industry that your business idea is associated with. You have to understand if the market that you are entering is growing or declining, and what are all the latest trends in the same industry. That will give you an idea of where you are really poised, as far as the industry you are planning to enter is concerned.

Research your 'target customers'

You might be catering to a particular niche and by researching your target audience based on factors like income levels and demographic factors, you will be able to get a solid idea of just how 'big' your target audience really is. The same goes if you are in the process of selling your goods online to a national or international audience; you have to understand the kind of numbers you are catering to out there.

Research your 'competition'

This is one of the most important things you could do. Make sure that you create a SWOT analysis so that you will be able to understand your competitors' strengths and weaknesses and how they might present opportunities and/or threats to your business. You might wish to keep an eye on that indirect competition out there, as well. For instance, if you're opening a fast food restaurant in a mall then you might wish to keep an eye on the fine dining restaurants in the mall as well, who might eat into that slice of 'pie' that you wish to carve out of the whole, for your very own.

Make sure you do those 'surveys'

Conducting surveys is one of the best possible methods that you could employ to understand what your potential customers out there really want; make sure that you use those online survey tools like SurveyMonkey and PollDaddy in order to get the best possible results. You could poll your customers on your website or even via email. The results that you accrue in this process will most certainly be most invaluable to you when it comes to getting valuable data for your business needs.

Have those 'focus groups'

Having a focus group is pretty much like doing a survey, but it is with a limited number of participants (usually not more than 10) and is far more in depth. You can ask those people in the focus group as to what they think about things like price points, advertising campaigns and service features. Of course you can have the meeting for up to 90 minutes, which helps you get more than the data you possibly need in order to understand that potential customer of yours. Of course you will have to pay them for their time, but you will see in time that it is well worth it!

Get help

Sometimes you will find that you might really get the best possible help from local colleges and universities. All you have to do is approach them for help and you might find that they are more than eager to do that market research for you as part of their research for a class project. You will be guaranteed a most high level of market research if they do.

Of course it is most important that a good deal of research be done before we even think of venturing out there in the business arena. It helps give you that much needed sense of clarity to move forward in the right direction and meet your business goals and objectives!

Chapter 3:

Step Three – The Business Plan

Now that you've done all the relevant market research that is needed to meet those business objectives of yours, the time has come to effectively plan your foray into the business arena so that you go through every step of the process in the best possible manner and with the least possible glitches.

Let's take a look at how we can effectively 'plan' our small business in order to take it forward.

In essence, this means that we have to create a business plan in order to ensure that we are highly consolidated in our approach to taking things forward and most prepared for any eventuality that might befall us during the course of taking that business of ours forward. Let's look at the things we need to keep in consideration when preparing the same.

You Must have a concise plan

Make sure that the plan is as concise as can possibly be, while at the same time ensuring that you do not miss any of the important details. If you're going to be showing that plan of yours to an investor, you really do need to trim all that fluff because it will only deter them from the process of reading it. So keep it to the point and simple.

Make sure that all the key areas are covered

You want to ensure that you do not miss any area that needs to be covered in that business plan of yours. Thus the areas like Company, Product/Service, Market, Competition, Management Team, Marketing, Operations and Financials should be covered in detail. Make sure that you use color charts and spreadsheets in order to make the relevant information presented in each of the sections far easier to understand.

Pay attention to the USP of your business

You have to convince the investor out there why it is indeed worth his or her salt to invest their money in that project of yours by showing them the USP (Unique Selling Proposition) of your product that will enable them to see just why that product or service of yours is worth investing in, as opposed to them merely keeping their money in a bank or investing in something like shares, in order for the same to grow.

Pay attention to those sales projections

While you will find that the costs are really rather easy to document, it is the sales projections that really need to be as conservative and realistic as possible. Make sure that you make a simple cash-flow and break even chart that will help you and anyone else who reads it gain a simple understanding into how many sales you need in order to cover your costs, and how much financing you need to raise in order to start up successfully.

The thing to remember here is that a lot of sales are on credit cards and that it might take up to four weeks to realize the cash thus collected; make sure you make those financial projections in tune with the same.

Executive Summary

Often this is presented at the beginning of the business plan and it is highly recommended that you do the same; but it is highly recommended that you begin the business plan with that executive summary because this is the thing that most investors will look to first, in an attempt to determine if they want to read further. They are strapped of time and so you need to make sure that this 'pitch' of yours strikes a solid punch and makes them thirsty for more. The executive summary in essence is nothing but a summary of that entire business plan of yours. It's like the plan in a nutshell.

Finally it must be emphasized that you really do need to stick to that business plan of yours, if you need to ensure that you are on the right path to success. That is because you have most clearly defined your business goals and objectives in it and thus it needs to be continually reviewed in order to ensure that you are indeed on the right track as far as it comes to implementing those goals and objectives.

Chapter 4:

Step Four – Getting Your Finances In Order

Now that you have your business plan ready, it's time to take things forward and set the ball rolling. Oh, did anyone mention that there might be money involved?

Of course, there will be!

Here's a look at the tips to ensure that your finances are up to the mark when it comes to funding your business endeavor.

Make sure that you budget your spending

You need to know how much money you need in order to break even and how much you need to spend in order to run your business on a daily basis. That budget of yours needs to be divided into four key areas: prospective income, fixed expenses, variable expenses and pay cheque-allowance. Make sure that you do not go overboard by having a good sense of balance between what you need and what you want.

Make sure that you invest well

You need to make sure that you invest that hard-earned money of yours on things that have long-term advantages. But of course you need to make sure that you balance well the cost against the return on the investment.

If the investment does not give you a significant return in terms of improving the quality of your business, then it might very well be worth revising your decision to make the same.

It is always better to 'invest' as opposed to 'spending' on things that will only give you benefits in the short term.

Make sure that you maintain those records well

A lot of times people find themselves at a loss to procure receipts of old simply because they did not take the effort to keep them in the first place. Make sure that you file away each and every receipt that might turn out to be helpful for you in the time to come.

You can also use an app that lets you upload your receipts and get access to an image of the receipt that you want whenever you want it, in that accounting system of yours.

Make sure that your personal and business bank accounts are kept separate

You will find that if you don't, it is easy to lose track of where that cash is coming from and you will find out much later on that you have been funding your business for some time through your own personal reserves. You might wish to avoid something like this happening by paying your business expenses with a dedicated business credit card with a fixed credit limit. This will give you the control to plan those cash in-flows of your business in order to meet those cash out-flows.

Cut down on those 'fixed' costs

It's really those 'fixed costs' that need to be worked on in an attempt to trim them, in order to ensure that that profitability of yours is not being eaten into. Thus you might wish to use 'Skype' instead of travelling long distances for those business meetings, whenever it is possible to do so. Or you might choose to use equipment that 'does the job' rather than procure fancy equipment that has way more features than you need and looks aesthetically more appealing. That way, you can make sure you cut down on unnecessary costs while at the same time ensuring there is no compromise at all in terms of the quality that is afforded to the customer out there.

Make sure that you create the right legal structure

When you're in the process of starting that small business of yours, you want in all probability to start out as a 'sole proprietor', because it really doesn't cost any money, as you don't have to pay to create corporate documents and tax returns. Of course, over the course of time you might have to change the structure of your business, depending on how it grows.

Make sure you get insurance if you need it

If you're operating out of your home, you won't really need it, but if you are operating from an office outside home, then you will need that minimum insurance on your office and assets.

Chapter 5:

Step Five – Choosing A Business Structure

In the previous chapter, we touched upon how we should create the right legal structure in order to ensure our finances are well taken care of; in this chapter, we will further explore this point in an attempt to understand exactly what kind of structure we need to assign to that fledgling business of ours, so that it can be primed in the best possible manner for success in the time to come. Let us take a look at the different types of business structures out there, with a view to understanding which one will work out best for us.

Types of Business Structures

A sole proprietorship, as earlier discussed, offers complete managerial control to the owner.

A partnership is a business structure that involves two or more people that agree to share in the profits and losses in a business.

A corporation is a legal entity that is created to conduct business. The corporation is an entity that is separate from the people that founded it.

LLC (Limited Liability Company) is a hybrid form of business structure that is increasingly gaining popularity. It allows the owners to take advantages of the perks afforded by both the partnership and corporation types of business structures.

Choosing a Business Structure

When it comes to the process of choosing a business structure from the ones that are outlined above, the following considerations need to be kept in mind.

Risks and Liabilities

In the case of your business providing services that are particularly risky, such as the trading of stocks, it would be most prudent to go in for an LLC, which will serve to protect your assets from business debts and claim. You might wish to go in for a 'corporation' type of structure, as well.

Formalities and Expenses

If you're starting a company on a shoestring budget, it is highly recommended that you go in for a sole proprietorship or a partnership. You do not wish to go in for an LLC here because it will be far more expensive to create and more difficult to maintain, as well. In the case of sole proprietorships and partnerships, however, you don't really have to fill in any forms or pay any fees in order to start your business. Also, there are no special operating rules out there that you are needed to follow.

Income Taxes

In the case of paying taxes, you will find that sole proprietorships, partnerships and LLCs all pay their taxes on business profits in the same way. All the profits and losses encountered herein pass from the business to the owners, who report their share of the profits on their personal income tax returns. The owners of these businesses must pay taxes on all the net profits of the business, irrespective of the amount of money they take out of the business each year.

However, the owners of a corporation pay taxes only on the profits they actually receive, such as in the case of bonuses, dividends and salaries. The corporation itself pays taxes at special corporate rates on the profits that are left in the company. And owing to the fact that corporations enjoy a lower tax rate than most individuals for the first $50000 to $75000 of corporate income, a corporation and its members might have a lower tax bill than that of the owners of an unincorporated business that earns the same level of profit.

Investment needs

Only a corporation will allow you to sell ownership shares in the company through those 'stock options' that makes it easier to procure investment and also retain employees within the organization. But if you are not envisaging your company to ever go public, you don't have to consider this option at all.

Of course there is no reason to believe that once you create the structure for your organization, it cannot be changed. You might start out small as a sole proprietorship or partnership and then as your business grows and your risk of liability increases, you might wish to convert it to an LLC or a corporation.

Chapter 6:

Step Six - Selecting And Registering Your Business Name

Now that you've chosen the appropriate business structure for the organization that you have proposed, you need to give it life by christening it with a name, right? Of course once that is done it will have to be registered as well, and then you will finally have the sense of your company being 'born', in the process. Let's take a look at all the steps that will be required to get us through the process.

Naming your small business

Of course the very first step would be to come up with a credible name for your business. You need to understand that having the right name is really most essential when it comes to your business; it might just provide that edge that you need over the competition, after all. Let's take a look on how we can effectively come up with a stellar business name.

Use a name that conveys a benefit

In case you are selling a product out there that you feel has a real tangible benefit that is its USP, you might wish to incorporate it as part of that product name, in order for it to have the desired effect on your target audience. In case you are opening an 'exotic' organic store, for example, you might wish to include the word 'exotic' as part of that name, for instance, so that you convey that which you are trying to sell out there in the most succinct fashion.

Use 'words' and not 'initials'

Unless you're a hugely successful corporation like IBM, initials won't do much towards portraying a rather stellar image of your brand out there. Make sure that you steer clear of them.

Make sure that it can be trademarked

You might wish to check up USTPO.gov before settling on the name that you have in mind. In case you are looking to make your brand big, you really need to make sure that the name can be trademarked.

Test it on Google AdWords

When you test the name you have shortlisted on Google AdWords, you get a list of similar search phrases along with how many global and monthly searches each is getting. This will also help to ensure that there is not a slightly similar word that will get far more attention than yours on the Internet.

Registering your Small Business Name

Now that you have gotten hold of an appropriate name for your small business, the time has come to register it so that you can finally move ahead with your business plans. In the case of having a sole proprietorship, you will find that it is not required to register your business name at the state level.

However, many states require that sole proprietors use their own name for the business until they formally file another name. This is known as your DBA (Doing

Business As). However, in the case of a corporation, limited liability company or even partnership you will find that you will have to register your business name with the State. This will ensure that no other corporation, limited liability company or partnership out there will be able to use the name that you have chosen.

Now that your official business name has been registered, if you want to sell products or services under a different name, then you have to file an assumed name certificate or a fictitious name statement. This is also needed if you want to use your LLC name without the suffix 'Limited Liability Company' or 'LLC'. In most states an LLC will file its fictitious name statement with the Secretary of State or Department of Corporations.

However, in some states the LLC needs to file a 'Doing Business As' certificate with the city clerk. In order to see where your LLC must file an assumed name certificate in your state, you have to go to the website of the 'U.S. Small Business Administration'.

Registering your business name as a trademark will ensure that no other business out there can take your name or one that's glaringly similar and you can do this with the U.S. Patent and Trademark Office.

Chapter 7:

Step Seven – Necessary

Licenses And Permits

Okay, so now you've gotten a name for that business of yours and even gone ahead and registered it out there in an attempt to get started as soon as you possibly can. So now what? Before you begin, there are certain things that you need to bear in mind, such as procuring the all important permits and licenses that are needed in order to make sure nothing gets in the way of your business when it is up and running. Let's take a look at all the licenses and permits that are required when it comes to running that small business of ours.

Business License

You need to contact your city's business license department and pay them a fee to procure that business license which grants you the permission to operate that business of yours in the city. What happens when you file that application for the license is, the city planning or zoning department will check to make sure that your area is zoned for the purpose that you wish to use it for and that there are enough parking spaces that are required to meet the codes.

In case an area is not zoned for your proposed business, then you will need to get a variance or a conditional-use permit. For that you will have to present your case before the city planning commission. As long as you show that your business will in no way disrupt the sanctity of the neighborhood where you propose to set up shop, it will be pretty easy to get that permit.

Fire Department Permit

You will have to get this one if your business involves the use of any flammable materials or if it will be open to the public. You will find that in some cities you have to get this permit even before you start your business; in others, all you have to do is schedule periodic inspections of your premises to ensure that they do indeed meet fire safety regulations.

Businesses that do the same include restaurants and day-care centers, places where a lot of people usually tend to congregate.

Air And Water Pollution Control Permit

In case your business involves the burning of materials, disposal of waste into sewers and even possibly involve the use of products that produce gas, you will need this permit.

Sign Permit

In some cities there are certain sign ordinances that restrict the size, location and even the type of lighting and sign that you might be using outside your business premises. You might wish to check with your landlord and get his or her written approval before you even think of putting that sign out there.

County Permits

If your business is located outside a city or town, these permits will be applicable to you. The county governments usually require the same kinds of licenses and permits that businesses need in cities, but at the same time the regulations in counties are not all that strict as those in cities.

State Licenses

In many states, you will find that people in certain occupations will be needed to have specific licenses or occupational permits. They might even have to pass state examinations before they can procure these licenses and start operating their businesses. These are generally applicable to people who provide personal services, such as insurance agents, barbers and cosmetologists.

Federal Licenses

There are a few businesses out there that require federal licenses, such as meat processors and radio and TV stations. The Federal Trade Commission will tell you if your business needs the same.

Sales Tax License

You need this 'certificate of resale' because any home-based business selling goods must pay taxes on the goods thus sold. In some states it's a criminal offense to operate without one, so make sure you get this before you open the doors to your business.

Health Department Permit

If you are in the business of supplying food to people either through a restaurant or through a wholesale business, you need this one. It costs around $25 and varies depending on the size of your business and the amount and size of the equipment you possess.

Chapter 8:

Step Eight - Location, Location, Location

Of course you've gotten a gist of all the licenses and permits that you will be needing when it comes to setting up your small business; what you need to bear in mind, though, is the fact that you might want to hold onto actually 'procuring' those licenses until you have found the absolute best location for your business.

The location of your business is integral in ensuring its success; you don't want to make a mistake by rushing in too soon and getting it wrong. Let's look at the ways in which we can ensure that we hit just the right 'spot' where it comes to finding that stellar location for our business.

Choose the most 'conducive' location

You have to do the obvious where it comes to choosing the right location, and that entails choosing one where there is increased consumer traffic in the case of the 'retailer' and one where there is easy access to suppliers and transport routes for the manufacturer. You cannot miss the obvious when it comes to securing the right location – make sure that you select a most conducive area to set up shop!

Make sure that it is 'financially' viable

No matter how great a location you might have zoned in on in an attempt to get the perfect spot for your business, it might not really be all that financially viable.

Remember, one must always keep their financial considerations first; you can settle for a less attractive area and keep that outstanding area that you have shortlisted for future reference.

Also, the property value is not the only thing that you need to bear in mind when securing your location; you have to be aware of the taxes as well. It might be significantly cheaper to operate in another city with more lenient taxation laws.

Of course the 'move' to another city might also mean that you have to charge less for your goods, so make sure you make this decision after giving it a good deal of thought.

Rent 'smart'

In the case of most businesses that are operating for the very first time in the field of retail, it might make a lot of sense to rent a space in a mall where you are ensured of a large number of footfalls. But you need to be warned – the rents might be so large that they can 'kill', and it might really be in your best interest to rent space in a mall that is not all that high end in the beginning, so that you don't pay all that much on rent.

Security

You have to ensure that the place you have selected is most 'safe'. The last thing you want is to put off customers by locating your business in a place where they are scared to venture into.

You need to make sure that you select a place that has a high level of security; one that will make both your team members and clients feel at ease.

Make sure that you inspect that property you have selected

You need to actually go out there and inspect the property that you have shortlisted, before you venture into a deal to secure the same. You have to see if looks as good in reality as it does on paper. Sometimes what you see and what you get can be two completely different things.

Play smart by locating next to the competition

Really? You might be thinking. Yes, that's just about the smartest move you could ever make. If you are in a business that deals in a specific industry such as travel, you might wish to locate in an area that is the proverbial 'Mecca' of the travel industry. That way half your work is already done; you will see that you get a lot more customers in the process than you would if you were located far away.

Think 'convenience'

If you are a family person then you would like your workplace close to home; if you are going to be using public transport you want a central location!

Chapter 9:

Step Nine - Choosing An Accounting System

Now that you're secure in the location your business needs to be in, you might want to take a look 'within' and scrutinize that business itself; it often involves a lot of mundane clerical work that is most efficiently managed by some top notch accounting software that you can choose to meet your accounting needs.

You will find that you will save a lot of time and have far more accurate records, if you use that accounting software as opposed to doing things manually.

Let's take a look, then, at the things we need to bear in mind when choosing that accounting system.

Narrow down those software choices

You can do this by taking stock of the services that are offered by the accounting systems out there, and choosing one that is best suited to your needs.

You will find that most of the accounting systems cover the following features.

\# Inventory management

\# Sales tracking

\# Managing customer contacts

\# Merchant account support to accept credit card payments

\# Budgeting

\# Estimates

\# Payroll

\# Business tax reporting

Industry-specific accounting systems

You have to keep in mind that there are certain accounting systems out there that are especially tailored for the kind of industry that you find yourself in. It might be a smart move to go in for one of these.

Thus if you find yourself in diverse fields like manufacturing and wholesale, you will find that there are software packages that are customized to cater to each one of these in a way that the individual requirements are met in specific and not covered in general like through certain accounting systems out there.

Talk to others

You will find other people in the same industry as yours using accounting software; make sure that you talk to them about the perks and disadvantages of the accounting software they use. That will help you make a choice far easier when it comes to zoning down on the best accounting software for your needs.

At the same time you will come to realize that there is really no software that is perfect; there are simply those that are better suited to your needs than others. Make sure that you talk to as many people as you possibly can about their accounting systems before you come your decision.

Find out whether it will grow with your business

You need to know if the software that you are looking at has modules that can be incorporated into it at a later stage; a common module that is incorporated in later stages is that of 'payroll accounting'.

In case the module cannot be added, you want to ensure that the accounting software is capable of being upgraded to a more efficient version, easily.

It should be compatible with your bank

You want to ensure that the accounting software that you have chosen works with your bank, because of the ease with which transactions can be downloaded from your bank, saving you a lot of time in the process.

Choosing between online and desk accounting software

Online software is the kind of accounting software that runs securely through a web browser. It is especially suited to those who are accessing accounting data and records from multiple computers, as opposed to the other 'desk accounting' type of software.

Can that access be restricted?

You might want one person to have absolute control over that accounting software in the sense that he or she can access all its areas; however, you might wish to afford some level of control to others in the organization to things like data entry.

At the same time you might not want them to have access to those 'reports' and you need to make sure that there is a system in place whereby you can give them 'selective access' to the software, thereby restricting their access to the same.

Does it come with a free trial?

You don't quite know how the software is going to actually 'work' until you have tried it; getting access to a free trial might be just the thing you need to nail your decision!

Chapter 10:

Step Ten - Promoting And Marketing Your Small Business

Of course, this final 'best' step is probably the one you've been waiting for all this while; that's why it is indeed kept to the very 'last'. It is well understood that to run any business successfully you really do need to have a solid marketing plan in place. That's what's going to give you that much needed 'edge' out there, after all, as far as taking your business to greater zeniths is concerned.

Let's get started, then, at uncovering just how we can effectively 'market' our business in order to meet those unparalleled levels of success that we have only dreamed of all this while.

Give it away for free!

Really? You might be thinking, how am I supposed to make any profit if I give my stuff away for free? Well of course you won't be doing it forever. Once you get those customers out there the opportunity to sample your product or service by offering it for free, they might just appreciate it to the extent that they convert to using yours over that which they have been accustomed to over time. In all probability you will get a lot more customers to try your product for the very first time if you happen to offer it 'free' to them, and that can dramatically increase the number of customers in that customer base of yours!

Be consistent in that e-mail campaign

You would want to ideally send an e-mail out to your valued customers once every week, wherein you provide something of 'value' to them. That is one of the best ways to remain connected with them and remind them of your presence, while at the same time showing them that you are dedicated to serving them with the highest standards of quality.

Try unusual marketing methods

If you choose to go the conventional route when advertising your product or services out there, you will find that you might end up spending a lot more money than you could afford. Often a most effective option is considering alternative advertising – for example, you could print an ad on a postcard and mail it to all the prospects in your area. You will be amazed at how many sales leads to your website you will generate in the process in a very short span of time and at virtually no cost.

Go in for joint promotions with other small business

You can offer to promote other small businesses out there to your customer database. In return, of course, you would expect those other small businesses to do the very same for you. This can be a great way to break into a market that would otherwise be largely untapped.

Create special deals for your existing customers

It is your existing customers that really give you the maximum business and not new customers out there; you want to ensure that you create special deals for them that will help them gain all the more confidence in your product or service and make them want to stick to using the same over time. It will make them feel special; now who on earth doesn't like to feel special every now and then?

You can even develop incentives for them that will ensure that they get rewarded with things like discounts every time they refer you to a friend of theirs.

Offer a premium version of your product or service

Once those existing customers discussed in the point above have decided to use your product or service, you might want to offer them a premium version of the same that they would be more than happy to lay their hands on, thus increasing your levels of profitability.

You could also introduce a 'package deal' whereby they could get an overall discount if they combined several products or services together. That would ensure that it would increase that 'transaction value' of theirs, meaning that you would make a lot more money in the process than you would were they to spend on a single product or service that you had to offer.

Conclusion

Over the course of this book we have seen just how the 'small' things in life can really be the 'biggest' by observing how we can leverage that small business idea of ours into fruition and maximize on our levels of profitability by ensuring that we reach those ambitious levels of success that all entrepreneurs dream of in the fledgling stages of business.

Thanks to the stellar tips provided in this book, you have seen that those dreams do not have to remain mere 'dreams', but can very well be converted to realities if you follow the basic principles that are firmly etched into this book.

The ten 'steps' that are outlined in this book are really most essential when it comes to working towards those entrepreneurial dreams of yours. If you follow them to the core we will find that it is really not all that difficult to make that business 'larger than life', even though in essence it might be 'small.'

Are you ready, then, to take charge of the dynamic process of working towards that small business dream of yours that has been harboring in your mind for ages?

Well, go on then, make it happen!

I will be more than happy to learn how this book has helped you in some way. If you feel you have learned something or you think it offered you some value, please take a moment to leave an honest review on Amazon. It would help many future readers who will be forever grateful to you. As I will!

To Your Success,
Adam Richards

DISCLAIMER AND/OR LEGAL NOTICES:
Every effort has been made to accurately represent this book and it's potential. Results vary with every individual, and your results may or may not be different from those depicted. No promises, guarantees or warranties, whether stated or implied, have been made that you will produce any specific result from this book. Your efforts are individual and unique, and may vary from those shown. Your success depends on your efforts, background and motivation.
The material in this publication is provided for educational and informational purposes. Use of the programs, advice, and information contained in this book is at the sole choice and risk of the reader.

CPSIA information can be obtained at www.ICGtesting.com
Printed in the USA
LVOW07s0425071115

461524LV00030B/940/P